Making the Most of Your Relationships

melody carlson

by design book 3

THINK

TH1NK
P.O. Box 35001
Colorado Springs, Colorado 80935

TH1NK is an imprint of NavPress.
TH1NK and the TH1NK logo are registered trademarks of NavPress. Absence of ® in connection with marks of NavPress or other parties does not indicate an absence of registration of those marks.

ISBN 13: 978-1-57683-727-6
ISBN 10: 1-57683-727-0

Published in association with the literary agency of Sara A. Fortenberry.

Cover design: Disciple Design
Cover illustration: Collins Dillard, Disciple Design
Creative Team: Gabe Filkey (s.c.m.), Nicci Jordan, Karen Lee-Thorp, Darla Hightower, Arvid Wallen, Glynese Northam

Printed in the United States of America

2 3 4 5 6 7 8 9 10 / 12 11 10 09 08

contents

introduction

*D*o you ever wonder *how you fit in?* Or whether you even do? Do you ever get frustrated by relationships? Whether it's a sibling who drives you bonkers, a best friend who sometimes acts like your worst friend, or a boyfriend who says one thing then does something totally different — relationships are usually a serious challenge!

In *Making the Most of Your Relationships* you will find Bible-based answers to these and many other sticky relationship questions. Not only that, but you'll probably pick up a few tools for de-stressing some of your relationships.

The bottom line is that God designed you to *need* people in your life — and he designed people to *need* you. And while the best things don't always come easily, the payoff is usually worth the trouble. So come along and find out how you can improve your life by *Making the Most of Your Relationships*!

about this series

*T*he *By Design* series was created to help you experience God's Word in a fun, fresh, and personal way. *Knowing God Better Than Ever* is a great book to start with since it's pretty basic and foundational. The topics of the other three books (*Making the Most of Your Relationships, Finding Out Who You Really Are,* and *Discovering a Forgiveness Plan*) were selected for how they specifically relate to what's going on in your life and can be used in any order that appeals to you.

how to use this book

There are several ways to use this book. You can do it with a group or on your own, whichever way works best for you. But sometimes it's easier to stick with something when you do it with friends. And it can be more fun too. If that's the case, you should pick a specific day and time when you'll meet (once a week) to go over that week's chapter together. You should also decide who will take the role of group leader (this helps to keep things rolling in the right direction).

And, naturally, everyone should read and do the writing assignments before getting together. Then when you meet, you can go over the chapter, share your answers or questions, things you've learned, goals you've made, goals you've attained, or goals you've blown (no one's perfect). And always make sure you pray for each other during the week. After six weeks, you will not only have completed this Bible study book but you'll feel a lot closer to your friends too.

As you go through each week's chapter, you can decide what pace works best for you. Some will want to read just a few pages each day, taking time to soak it in and carefully complete the assignments. Others may prefer to do one whole chapter at a sitting—but if that's the case, make sure you go back over it during the rest of the week (consider the Bible verses or goals you've made).

Mostly, you need to discover which way works best for you, then stick with it. And hopefully, as you work through this series, you'll appreciate how God's Word really does have meaning and practical guidance for your life.

the stuff of life — *people!*

We, though, are going to love—love and be loved.

First we were loved, now we love. He loved us first.

1 John 4:19

ave you ever noticed that no matter what you do, where you go, where you live, it's difficult to get away from people—well, at least for very long anyway. The planet is jam-packed with them and the numbers are increasing by the second. Seriously, people are everywhere you look. They're bumping up against you at school or where you work. They're taking up air space at the mall or in your house. It's like you're totally surrounded!

And that's just what God intended. He wants you to be surrounded. That's because he specifically designed you with a real need to be around certain people—and he designed certain people with a real need to be around you.

Even so, that doesn't make it easy, does it? In fact, unless you're very unusual, you probably find it pretty challenging at times. That's because the people in your life equal relationships, and relationships get sticky. People let you down and you get hurt. Then you let them down and they get mad. It's bound to happen. But that's also what God intended.

God knows that nothing else can shape and refine your life as much as interacting with all those people he's so strategically placed all around you. Say you see a need for patience in yourself—maybe you even pray for it—and the next thing you know you are paired up with the most obnoxious jerk for your new lab partner. Is it a coincidence? Or is it God giving you an opportunity to be changed into the kind of person who reflects his image?

So, like it or not, people are here to stay. And God's plan for you is to get in there and make the most of these relationships. And while you're doing that, God will be making the most of you! Not a bad deal, if you think about it.

But you, dear friends, carefully build yourselves up in this most holy faith by praying in the Holy Spirit, staying right at the center of God's love, keeping your arms open and outstretched, ready for the mercy of our Master, Jesus Christ. This is the unending life, the real life!

Jude 1:20-21

Your Best Best Friend

God knows that being a really good friend doesn't come naturally to most people. He knows that by nature you're probably a little self-centered. Even if you try to hide it, God understands. He knows the way humans operate.

That's one of the reasons he sent Jesus to earth. He wanted mankind to have an example of what it takes to be a really good friend — the best best friend anyone could ever wish for. And Jesus invited everyone to follow his example.

The best way for you to learn how to be a Jesus-kind-of-friend is to spend time with him and make him your very best best friend. Because the truth is, the people you hang with do rub off on you — eventually. And Jesus wants you to learn from him as you make it your goal to get better at this relationships game.

lisa chan's story

"Yeah, whatever," I say into my cell phone. I'm trying my best to act nonchalant, like I could care less that my best friend — make that my ex-best friend — is blowing me off again. It's like the third time this week she's made up some pathetic excuse when I've invited her to do something with me. "I figured you'd be busy."

"It's not that — "

"Then what is it, Shelby?" I demand, totally ruining my no-big-deal act. "Why don't you want to do anything with me anymore? Why are you treating me like we're not even friends? I just don't get it." I can feel tears at the corners of my eyes now, and I hope she can't hear the choke at the end of my sentence.

"Hey, I'm sorry, Lisa." She's using this weird sort of disconnected voice that doesn't even sound like her now. "It's just that I've been hanging with Mattie a lot more lately — we're both really getting into debate team. And then there's Peter, you know, we're starting to get more serious. I'm just busier than I used to be."

"Yeah, whatever." I realize I've used this line about four times already and I know it's getting old. "Sorry to bother you."

"Don't be all mad at me, Lisa."

"Don't tell me how to feel, Shelby."

"I'm not."

"Yeah, whatever." Great, that makes five times. "I'll talk to you later."

"Yeah, later."

I hang up. But I know there won't be a later. I can just feel it inside of me. This friendship is over. That's when I really start to cry.

But after I quit crying, I make a decision. I do not need friends. Plain and simple. Friends are just a great big pain in the behind, and I'll probably be better off without them. I was totally shattered when I lost my best friend Megan Phillips a couple of years ago. We'd been friends since grade school and had even promised to be maids of honor at each other's weddings. But she forgot all about that and me when she got all popular at the beginning of freshman year. That hurt a lot.

But it wasn't long after that that Shelby and I became friends. We were both feeling like loners and started hanging together in journalism class and then during lunch, and before long we were pretty much inseparable. Of course, this helped me forget all about Megan. Well, mostly. I still missed the fun times we had back in middle school when she wasn't so obsessed with being Miss Cool Chick. But I didn't dwell on it. I just put my energy into being the best friend I could be to Shelby. And let me tell you that wasn't exactly easy. Shelby is what some people might call a "high-maintenance" person. In other words, she's pretty needy.

But she seemed to appreciate my efforts. And, naturally, I appreciated having a best friend again. It was like we needed each other. The thing is,

I've totally been there for Shelby. Like when her parents started having marriage problems during our sophomore year, I was always there to listen to her. Then when Todd King broke up with her last year, after six months of going out, whose shoulder did she cry on for days and days? She's even been known to call me up late at night when she's freaked out over something as trivial as getting a zit on her chin the day before class pictures were taken. And, of course, I would listen and reassure her that a little zit-cream before bed, and some cover-up the next morning, and everything would be fine. And it was.

But did I ever call her about something as stupid as that? Of course not. Shelby wasn't exactly the kind of friend who had patience with the imperfections of others. Probably just one more reason that she's so into Mattie Cavanaugh now. Mattie is one of those girls who manages to work her way into whichever crowd suits her. She's captain of the debate team and fairly academic without being a nerd.

Whereas Shelby and I nearly fell into the nerd category since we're both pretty academic and really into journalism, yearbook, and the school paper. Things that some kids (like Megan) don't really respect and sometimes even make fun of. But it didn't hurt so much when I had Shelby by my side. It's like I felt protected somehow. Now I feel abandoned and betrayed.

By the time I get ready for bed, I've decided that I've had it with Shelby. Let her see if Miss Perfect Mattie Cavanaugh will give a rip if Shelby gets a zit at midnight. See if she puts up with Shelby's constant draining neediness. I gave Shelby my best effort at being a really good best friend. If that's not good enough for her, well, FINE!

And as I get into bed, I decide that I've had it with friends in general. I mean, first Megan then Shelby stabbed me in the back. Who needs them *anyway? From now on I'm going solo. I don't want their friendship any more than they want mine. Period.*

1. What is Lisa trying to get or avoid by giving up on friends?

[Jesus said:] "Walk with me and work with me—watch how I do it. Learn the unforced rhythms of grace. I won't lay anything heavy or ill-fitting on you. Keep company with me and you'll learn to live freely and lightly."

Matthew 11:29-30

Matter of Trust

Do you believe God really has your best interests at heart? Do you think he cares enough about you to put certain things into place that will help to make you into the person he wants you to become? If you really believe those things, it's time to look around you — it's time to see the people God has placed in your life — and it's time to begin trusting him for those relationships.

Maybe you have parent issues. Who doesn't? Do you think God made a mistake by allowing you to be born into that family? Not. God knows all about you and your parents, and he has a plan that's way beyond anything you could hope for. But his plans won't evolve without your full cooperation.

Maybe there's a person that is driving you bonkers—a so-called friend who's anything but friendly, or a teacher who seems to think you're her whipping girl. Whatever challenging relationships you face, you need to put them into God's hands. You need to trust that he is up to something—something good and in your best interest.

Getting Honest

2. How do you feel about your relationships in general? Rank yourself on a scale of 1 to 10 (1 = they totally suck and 10 = I love everyone and everyone loves me). Then briefly explain why you picked that number.

3. Do you see God more as:
   a. Your heavenly Father
   b. A stern judge
   c. Your best friend
   d. Someone you'd like to get to know better
   e. Other: _____
   Explain your choice.

4. Can you accept that God has placed certain people around you for a purpose? Pick one person and write why you need that person in your life.

5. List five things you expect from a friend.

6. Are you willing to become that for a friend? Why or why not?

7. Think of a difficult person in your life. How could God change you through this person?

Play It Forward

Jesus said, "Love your neighbor as you love yourself." Pretty simple, isn't it? But, as you know, simple isn't always easy. And Jesus was well aware of that since he was born in a time when hatred reigned because of religious and cultural differences (not so unlike the Middle East today). So when Jesus was asked, "Who is my neighbor?" he told his audience the story of a Jewish man and a Samaritan (a group that most Jews saw as bad both ethnically and religiously:

"There was once a man traveling from Jerusalem to Jericho. On the way he was attacked by robbers. They took his clothes, beat him up, and went off leaving him half-dead. Luckily, a priest was on his way down the same road, but when he saw him he angled across to the other side. Then a Levite religious man showed up; he also avoided the injured man.

"A Samaritan traveling the road came on him. When he saw the man's condition, his heart went out to him. He gave him first aid, disinfecting and bandaging his wounds. Then he lifted him onto his donkey, led him to an inn, and made him comfortable. In the morning he took out two silver coins and gave them to the innkeeper, saying, 'Take good care of him. If it costs any more, put it on my bill—I'll pay you on my way back.'

"What do you think? Which of the three became a neighbor to the man attacked by robbers?"

(Luke 10:30-36)

Ask Yourself . . .

8. What am I supposed to get out of Jesus' story about the Samaritan?

9. Do I find some people easier to love than others? Why is that?

10. Am I resistant to loving people who are different from me? Why or why not?

11. Is there someone in my life right now who I really don't want to love? If so, who? And why?

12. My prayer for the "unlovable" people in my life:

lisa's story continues . . .

It's been a week since I started my solitude routine. And in some ways it's been okay. I mean, I don't have to worry about someone asking to borrow something, and I don't get phone calls interrupting me while I'm doing my homework. I don't even have to act nice when I don't feel like it.

But here's the downside: I am kinda lonely. Oh, I'm getting really good at not showing it. I walk around with what I think is sort of an I'm-just-fine-thank-you-very-much expression on my face. I go about my life without getting involved in anyone else's. It's like I'm in my own little world. But then I heard Tina Millagro say that I've turned into a big snob. Of course, she didn't know that I was behind the closed door of the bathroom stall at the time. And I didn't come out until she and her friends were long gone. The thing that hurt about that is that Tina goes to my church and I thought she would know better than that. But I guess it just helps to prove my point. People will eventually hurt and betray you, and it's better to keep a distance and not trust them.

I think I might get a cat. I saw a sign on my way home from school today: "Free Kittens." Maybe I can have a cat for a friend.

"Are you going to youth group tonight?" my mom asks me as I'm grabbing a snack to take to my room.

"I don't think so," I tell her, already making my way to the door.

"Why not?"

"*Uh, I have homework,*" I say. *Not untrue, but not the reason for not going.*

"*That's never stopped you before.*"

"*I know. I guess I just don't feel like it.*"

Her face softens now. "*Are you feeling okay, Lisa? You seem awfully quiet lately.*"

"*I'm fine,*" I lie.

"*We haven't seen much of Shelby around? Is she okay?*"

"*She's fine. Just busy.*"

"*Oh.*" *She frowns and I can tell she suspects something.*

"*It's okay,*" I say quickly.

Then to change the subject, I ask if I can get a cat, and to my total surprise she actually agrees. Usually she thinks pets are a messy nuisance.

"*Just know that you have to take care of it, Lisa,*" *she says finally.*

"*Yeah, that's the point,*" I tell her. "*I think it'll be fun to take care of it.*"

I also think that a cat, unlike a person, should like me for who I am. And if I feed and care for my cat, I'm guessing my cat will be loyal and stick around. And that's more than you can say for some people!

"I'm telling you to love your enemies. Let them bring out the best in you,
not the worst. When someone gives you a hard time,
respond with the energies of prayer, for then you are working
out of your true selves, your God-created selves. This is what God does.
He gives his best—the sun to warm and the rain to nourish—to everyone,
regardless: the good and bad, the nice and nasty."

Matthew 5:44-45

What About This?

13. List three ways you think an "enemy" could "bring out the best" in you.

14. How do you feel when something really great happens to someone you dislike?

15. How do you think God wants you to feel?

Full Circle

Okay, the first part of Jesus' commandment was "to love others," but the second part was "as you love yourself." What do you think that was supposed to mean? Was Jesus suggesting that you should invest as much time and energy into doing things for others as you do for yourself?

Maybe that's a part of it, but maybe there's more. Maybe there's a hidden clue here. Maybe Jesus wanted to get you thinking.

Do you love yourself? Answer that question honestly. Do you really love yourself? Do you look in the mirror and smile and say, "I love you!"? Okay, probably not, since that would be just a little weird. But, on the other hand, do you ever look in the mirror and say, "I hate you"? Or do you ever say to yourself, "I am so stupid!"? That's not very loving, is it?

Maybe Jesus' point was to get you to the place where you really do love and accept yourself — in the same way that God loves and accepts you — and then something amazing happens. You are changed! You suddenly see the world and the people around you differently. You don't feel nearly as threatened or irritated or hostile toward them as you did before. And that's because the way you feel about yourself is directly reflected in the way you respond to others.

It's a fact that people with low self-esteem tend to treat others poorly, while people with good self-esteem tend to treat others with respect. Maybe that's what Jesus was getting at.

What About It?

16. Do you think Lisa (in the story) loves herself? Why or why not?

17. Do you think you love yourself? Why or why not?

Words to Live By

(Consider memorizing this.)

If all you do is love the lovable, do you expect a bonus?
Anybody can do that. If you simply say hello to those who greet you,
do you expect a medal? Any run-of-the-mill sinner does that.
"In a word, what I'm saying is, Grow up. You're kingdom subjects.
Now live like it. Live out your God-created identity.
Live generously and graciously toward others,
the way God lives toward you."

Matthew 5:46-48

Journal Your Thoughts

Consider Matthew 5:46-48. Journal below what those words mean to you. How do they challenge you?

My Relationship Goals

Okay, you've only begun this book, but it's time to write down some goals. This is your way to take some control in designing your life. And don't worry if your goals are a bit vague to start with. Like you might just say, "I want to learn how to be a better friend," or "I want to learn how to choose better friends," or "I want to love myself more." Just do the best you can with what you've learned so far. By the end of the book, your goals will probably change a lot anyway.

My Beginning Goals Are:

God's People Plan

So, maybe you're starting to see that it's no random thing that your life is surrounded by such an interesting cast of characters. Maybe you suspect that God really is up to something, and perhaps you're even beginning to feel hopeful about some of the relationship challenges you're facing. Answer the following questions and you have completed chapter 1!

18. List five people in your life who you consider to be God's gifts to you. Then write one or more attributes (like thoughtful, kind, generous, encouraging) by each name.

19. List five people in your life who (until now) you thought you could live without. Then write at least one positive attribute by each name. Okay, it won't be easy, but try.

20. Now list your strengths as a person and a friend.

21. Use the space below to write a prayer inviting God to change your thinking about the relationships in your life.

"I've never quit loving you and never will.

Expect love, love, and more love!

And so now I'll start over with you and build you up again . . .

You'll resume your singing, grabbing tambourines

and joining the dance."

Jeremiah 31:3-4

it's all
relative

Honor your father and mother so that you'll live a long time
in the land that GOD, your God, is giving you.

Exodus 20:12

*Y*ou can choose your friends, but you're pretty much stuck with your family. And while there may be times when you actually appreciate your relatives, you still probably experience those moments when you wonder if some devious maternity ward nurse pulled off a baby swap on the day you were born. Because, it's a fact, family members can really get to you.

But if you're trusting God for the arrangement of the people in your life, you've got to trust him for your family as well. Oh, that's not to say there aren't some families where things have gone so totally wrong that they ultimately self-destruct, leaving members scattered and hurt. But that was never God's intention for them — it was most likely the result of ongoing bad choices and sin. And, of course, there are also those families that split apart as a result of divorce, and while that's a painful time, God is able to bring good out of it too — if you allow him.

Whatever the case with your situation, you might as well accept that no family, including yours, is flawless. And while you may know someone who seems to have lucked out with the "perfect" family, be assured, they too have their troubles. Some are just better at keeping them hidden. In fact, keeping things hidden is often a symptom of serious problems. The difference between a "functional" family and a "dysfunctional" one is that both families have this metaphorical pile of crud on the floor, but the dysfunctional family tries to cover the stinking heap with a pretty rug and a coffee table, while the functional family gets out the shovels and attempts to clean it up.

In other words, the only way to make a family work is to be open and honest and to deal with things as they happen. If you allow the crud to pile up, it's a whole lot harder to clean up later.

And maybe this is one reason God designed families in the first place: Your family is your training ground for future relationships. The good news is that even though you blow it with your family, they almost have to forgive you. Because, after all, you're family — they gotta love you.

> Friends love through all kinds of weather,
> and families stick together in all kinds of trouble.
> Proverbs 17:17

Home School of Hard Knocks

So how do you react when your younger sister borrows your new jacket and returns it with a hole in the sleeve? What do you say when your older brother swipes your favorite shampoo and doesn't return it? And what happens when your dad teases you in front of your new friend and you suddenly feel like you're about six years old again? Or what if you and your mom disagree on the outfit you've painstakingly put together for the dance?

Home is the testing ground for dealing with hard stuff. You can either let family squabbles totally frustrate you, or you can try to learn from these challenges and start showing some real maturity. Oh, sure, it's not easy growing up. And sometimes you wish everyone around you would just grow up themselves. But the only person you can truly control is yourself. How are you going to handle it?

One way to start understanding why you react the way you do at home is to consider your placement in the birth order. For instance, firstborn children tend to take on more responsibility — the upside is that parents usually trust them more; the downside is that they can be pretty bossy to their younger siblings. Second-born children are usually a bit competitive, feeling they have to prove themselves — the upside is that they're more independent; the downside is that they can become rebellious. The "baby" in the family is used to getting more attention and learns how to work the system — the upside is they learn from siblings' mistakes; the downside is they can be a little lazy and spoiled. And the one without siblings, an only child, is often a combination of a firstborn and the "baby." The upside is they might be more mature and responsible; the downside is they might be spoiled and demanding.

Okay, these are some pretty general generalizations, and no one ever falls completely into one category, but it might help you understand the dynamics of your family when you begin to see the role you've been handed and decide whether or not you want to keep playing it.

What Do You Think?

1. Where do you fit in the birth order of your family? What do you see as your strengths or weaknesses?

2. How do you think your family perceives you? How would they describe you?

3. Describe your reaction mode when someone in your family does something that aggravates you. Do you flare up? Clam up? Or just pretend not to care?

4. On a scale of 1 to 10, how would you describe your family's ability to communicate? (1 = we never talk, 10 = we can and do talk to each other about anything and everything.)

5. Why do you think your family is at this level? Are you happy with it?

6. If you could change one thing about the way you interact with your family, what would it be? And how would you go about it?

lisa's story continues . . .

I wait until Friday to get my kitten. The little old lady who owns the mother cat is surprised when I choose the runt of the litter. She actually tries to talk me out of it.

"Oh, dear, why don't you take one of the black-and-white kitties instead?" she urges me. "That little tiger cat might not be that healthy."

I shake my head as I cuddle the tiny kitten close to my chest. "No," I tell the lady, "this kitten needs me."

"Well, that may be," she says, "but these black-and-whites are awfully cute."

"Thanks, but no thanks," I tell her. Then I write down some instructions for caring for my kitty and go home.

I name my kitten Clarice. I have no idea why, it just seems to fit her. Then I take her to Petco and get all kinds of things for her. It's the most fun I've had in weeks. Okay, I know how pathetic that makes me sound. But it's the truth.

And now I have her home and all set up in my bedroom, and I'm actually feeling a little less lonely. Too bad Clarice can't talk. Even so, she's a good listener.

"I know how you feel, Clarice," I tell her as I set up her kitty litter box, which she immediately puts to good use. The cat lady told me that the mama cat already taught the little ones how to do this. That's a relief. "You were the runt of the litter, the one who looked different, the one the others pushed aside." I reach down and stroke her soft coat. "That's a lot like me."

I put her on my bed with me and continue to talk. I tell her about how it's hard being Asian in a school that's primarily Caucasian. I tell her how it feels to be without friends. How I get pretty lonely sometimes. "But it's better this way," I finally say. "This way I won't keep getting hurt. Besides, I have you now."

Later that evening, my sister Katy comes home from college. "You got a kitten?" she asks with astonishment.

"Yeah," I hold up Clarice for her to see.

"Mom never let me have a kitten." She frowns at Clarice as if this is my poor kitten's personal fault. "She always said pets were too messy."

"Well, she must've changed her mind about that."

"That's because you're the baby, Lisa. Mom and Dad always let you have your way."

"They do not."

"Oh, puh-leeze. You know they do. Ever since you were born, you've gotten away with everything."

"I have not."

"Yeah, right." She rolls her eyes and then heads to the kitchen. I want to scream at her, to tell her she's totally wrong, and why doesn't she act her age instead of her shoe size for a change! But then I wonder, what's the use? Besides, I tell myself, why should I care? I'm the one who doesn't need anyone. And I certainly don't need a bossy know-it-all big sister. Why waste my energy even thinking about it? Then I take Clarice to my room and close the door and consider staying there all weekend. Maybe even for the rest of my life.

Israel loved Joseph more than any of his other sons because he was the child of his old age. And he made him an elaborately embroidered coat. When his brothers realized that their father loved him more than them, they grew to hate him—they wouldn't even speak to him.

Genesis 37:3-4

What About This?

7. Maybe you've heard the story of Joseph, the young man who was sold as a slave by his jealous brothers (Genesis 37). Do you think there's jealousy among the siblings in your family? If so, describe it.

8. What's one thing you'd like to change about the way you interact with a sibling?

I Need Some Help!

Okay, so maybe you're seeing that you have some growing up to do when it comes to your family relationships. Or maybe, like Lisa, you think someone else in your family needs to grow up. Whatever the case, you've probably felt like giving up from time to time. Maybe you feel like it's hopeless even now — like things are so messed up that it'll never get better.

In some ways, that's not a bad place to be. Sometimes you need to feel your back against the wall before you become desperate to really cry out to God for help. And you know what? When you cry out, he's always ready to answer. Oh, you might not like his answer at first, but if you trust him, you might appreciate it in time.

God wants you to admit your inability to successfully handle relationships with your own strength. He knows your weaknesses (after all, he created you!), and he wants you to bring your weaknesses to him and invite him to help you. He also wants to empower you with his Holy Spirit — God's strength dwelling within you. All you need to do is just ask — and trust that he will answer.

Ask Yourself . . .

9. List five specific things about your family that really stress you out.

10. Do you think your way of interacting with family members pleases God? Why or why not?

11. What do you think God is trying to say to you regarding your family relationships? Be specific.

> "My grace is enough; it's all you need.
> My strength comes into its own in your weakness."
> Once I heard that, I was glad to let it happen.
> I quit focusing on the handicap and began appreciating the gift.
> It was a case of Christ's strength moving in on my weakness.
>
> 2 Corinthians 12:9

12. Which family situation makes you feel the most helpless?

13. Write a prayer to God, asking for his help in this situation.

Communication Skills 101

You can't have good relationships without good communication. And don't be fooled, good communication isn't really about the words you speak. Real communication is about voice tone, facial expressions, body language, and finally the words.

Say your mom asks how you're doing, and you say, "Just fine." Well, maybe you really are just fine, but if your arms are crossed, your brows are pulled together, and there's a sarcastic tone in your voice, chances are you're really just angry. Or maybe you're just sending the wrong signals.

One of the biggest challenges in establishing good communication is realizing how you come across to others. Like, are people really getting you? And if not, why not? The following quiz might help you get a handle on your communication strengths or weaknesses.

does your family get you?

Circle the letter of the answer that fits your communication style best.

1. You're talking to your dad about whose turn it is to mow the lawn. Describe your body language.
   a. You cross your arms.
   b. You wave your hands around to make your point.
   c. You lean forward to listen better.

2. Your brother promised to take you to the mall and then didn't. When you see him:
   a. You pretend it's no big deal.
   b. You barely speak to him so he'll know you're ticked.
   c. You say, "How come you promised to take me to the mall then never showed up?"

3. Your sister asks you to lie about what time she got home last night. You say:
   a. "Uh, sure, whatever . . ."
   b. "Okay," but you avoid parents the next day.
   c. "I'm not okay with that."

4. You're talking to your dad about religion (but wishing he'd give you your allowance), when he says something you don't agree with. You:
   a. Pretend to agree and hope he's about to hand over the cash.
   b. Change the subject and hope he doesn't notice.
   c. Tell him you respect his opinion but don't really agree.

5. Your mom wants to "discuss sex" again. Are you able to look her in the eye?
   a. Not at all!
   b. Sometimes.
   c. Yeah, what's the big deal?

6. Your mom asks you to babysit for a friend of hers, but you don't want to. You say:
    a. "I guess so . . . if they really need me."
    b. "I sort of had other plans."
    c. "I'm sorry, but I'm not really into babysitting tonight."

7. Who does most of the talking in your family's conversations?
    a. You do — and they sometimes tease you about hogging the attention.
    b. The rest of your family takes over since you're not good at starting a conversation.
    c. It's pretty even; everyone gets their turn.

8. Your mom wants to know about the dress you want for the next dance. You describe it as:
    a. "It was like pale blue with, like, this yellow embroidery, ya know, around the skirt . . ."
    b. "It was pale blue with, like, this yellow embroidery around the skirt."
    c. "It was pale blue with yellow embroidery around the skirt."

Now count your answers and see which letter you chose most to find out if you're communicating as well as you think.

A. **Well, uh, not exactly . . .** Your communication is pretty vague. Your family is probably unsure about what you're thinking. Next time you feel yourself holding back in a situation, write down what you really wanted to say afterward and see how it compares. Then ask God to help you to speak more directly next time.

B. Sort of, maybe, sometimes . . . Your communication ability depends on the situation. If you're feeling comfortable, you communicate better. But if you're not, you tend to sort of bumble around. Next time you feel stumped about speaking your mind, take a deep breath, say a silent prayer, and answer honestly. It might feel awkward to start with, but it will pay off with communication confidence in time.

C. Absolutely, yes, you bet! You communicate directly and with ease. And, no doubt, your family is definitely getting you. Just make sure that you ask God to help you be a good listener so that you can get them too.

Words to Live By

(Consider memorizing this.)

Children, do what your parents tell you. This is only right. "Honor your father and mother" is the first commandment that has a promise attached to it, namely, "so you will live well and have a long life."

Ephesians 6:1-3

Journal Your Thoughts

Consider Ephesians 6:1-3. Write below about how you interact with your parents and whether you think this is pleasing to God or not.

My Relationship Goals for My Family

Hopefully this chapter has challenged you to see yourself and your place in your family with a fresh perspective. Glance back over your responses to the questions and quizzes and your journal entry, and see what stands out most to you. Then list some goals concerning your family.

My Goals Are:

Relax, everything's going to be all right;

rest, everything's coming together;

open your hearts, love is on the way!

Jude 1:2

totally lost without
them

It is better to have a partner than go it alone.
Share the work, share the wealth.
And if one falls down, the other helps,
But if there's no one to help, tough!

Two in a bed warm each other.
Alone, you shiver all night.

By yourself you're unprotected,
With a friend you can face the worst.
Can you round up a third?
A three-stranded rope isn't easily snapped.

Ecclesiastes 4:9-12

riends! How boring would life be without them? Oh, sure, friends will hurt you occasionally, but that's only because you really care about what they think. Most of the time, you're probably really glad to have them around. Even so, what do you do when a good friendship goes sideways?

Are there tricks to restoring broken friendships? Do you think there are some friendships that you're better off leaving behind? And others that you should fight for? And how do you know the difference?

Lisa is hurting because Shelby seemingly dumped her. But did she ever stop to ask Shelby if this was really a fact? Or did she ever ask Shelby why? Is it possible that Lisa did something to offend Shelby and doesn't even know it? And more important, has Lisa considered whether or not her friendship with Shelby is worth salvaging?

Lisa has convinced herself she can get by without friends. But how long do you think a person can last in that kind of isolation? How long could you last without a single friend? And do you think it's odd that Lisa doesn't seem to have any other friends? Was Shelby her only friend? If so, why?

If you're like most people, you still have some unanswered questions about friendships. Maybe you're in a frustrating friendship right now. In this chapter, you'll explore lots of friendship basics and hopefully learn not only how to have good friends but also how you can be one!

It's you! We grew up together! You! My best friend!
Those long hours of leisure as we walked arm in arm,
God a third party to our conversation.
Psalm 55:13-14

Levels of Friendship

Everyone wants a best friend—someone you can tell your secrets to, who will be there when you're brokenhearted, who will listen to you and give you dependable advice — a good best friend is worth more than the most expensive bling bling! But there's probably room in your life for more than just one single friend. And it's good to surround yourself with several good friends — it can even take the pressure off the friendship with your best friend. And it's more fun!

There are varying levels of friendship. And that's okay, because it would be really tricky to have, say, six *best* friends. Take a look at the three main levels of friendship and see where your friends fit in.

Best friend. This is the most limited category, meaning most people can't handle more than one or two best friends. In fact, one at a time is usually the easiest to manage. Your best friend is someone you have a lot in common with. She is most likely a Christian too, because you need someone who shares your basic values. She's someone you enjoy being with and can relax with. Someone who is a good listener, can be trusted with your deepest secrets, and is loyal. She's someone who can expect exactly the same things from you. In fact, she's a person you would do almost anything for. Hopefully she's a friend you will have in your life for years and years to come.

Close friends. This second category is really important but also limited. Most people can't manage more than five or six close friends without feeling overwhelmed — three or four are probably plenty. These are the girls you feel comfortable with, the girls who won't backstab you or gossip about you. You might not tell them your deepest secrets, but you can trust them to stand by you when you need them. These are the friends you join at the lunch table, go to the mall or a movie or youth group with, and call with a problem when your best friend is unavailable. Your close friends don't all have to be Christians, but you want them to have similar values, and you want them to be open to hearing about your faith. Close friends bring color and fun into your life, but you have a responsibility to return their friendship with the same kind of enthusiasm.

Casual friends. This is the unlimited category. You can never have too many casual friends. These are the kids you rub up against every day. Classmates, teachers, coworkers, youth group friends. You treat them with kindness and respect, and hopefully they give it back in return. These are *not* the people you tell your secrets to, *not* the people you trust your heart to, *not* the people you depend on when you're in a bind. Not that they can't deliver, but you just don't expect it from them. It's likely that many of your casual friends are not believers, but that's okay. God may be using you in their lives, and it's important to keep the friendship door open with them. And one good thing about casual friends is that they can always become close friends later on down the line.

Who Are Your Friends?

1. List the names of your friends under the category where you think they fit.

Best Friend(s)   **Close Friends**   **Casual Friends**

Now consider the balance of your list — like do you have tons of casual friends but no close friends? Do you like how your list looks?

lisa's story continues . . .

I finally leave my room on Sunday to go to church. It's easier than making up some excuse for my parents. Although I notice that Katy has slept in. Of course, she's in college and uses the "I'm so tired and don't get enough rest" routine — and my parents always fall for it. Yeah, right.

"Do you want to ride with us?" asks my dad. He asks the same thing every Sunday, and I give him my usual answer.

"Nah," I say. "I'd rather drive my own car in case I decide to do something afterward." Of course, I don't tell him that I really have absolutely nothing to do, or that Shelby probably won't be asking me to go to the mall with her, or that I'll probably just come straight home, back to my room and Clarice. But then he doesn't ask either.

I'm tempted to skip out on the high school worship and just go to the regular worship service, but I know this would probably make my parents suspicious, and I don't particularly care to explain my friendless situation to them. They'd only get worried and probably try to set me up for some kind of counseling. My dad's a psychologist and thinks everything can be solved with good counseling. So I just drive really slowly to church, take my time in the parking lot, and arrive at the youth house after the service has begun.

I sit in the back and pretend to sing, but my heart is not in it. I can see Shelby sitting up close to the front — the same row where she and I usually sit. I'm slightly surprised to see that Mattie is with her, because I know Mattie's not a Christian. Well, fine, I tell myself. That really cuts me out of the picture now.

The message (which blew right past me) is finished, and the youth leader is inviting us to bow our heads and pray, and suddenly I realize that it's been awhile since I talked to God honestly. And I feel kind of panicky as I wonder if my little solo plan included giving up my friendship with God as well. This actually worries me — a lot. So I really do pray, and I tell God that I'm sorry, and that I do want him as my friend. Even if he is my one and only friend. At least I know enough to realize that I can't get by without God. Me, God, and Clarice — maybe that's enough.

Finally the service ends and I head straight for the door. I keep my eyes downward so that I won't exchange glances with Shelby. No way do I want her to see me feeling this bummed — and all because of her. I won't give her the satisfaction of thinking how pathetic I look. I just shoot out the door and hurry to my car.

But as I go, I find that I'm praying. I'm asking God to help me to not feel so lonely. "You should be enough for me," I pray silently. "Help me to depend on you for more. Help me to make you into my very best friend."

And while my prayer is comforting (a little anyway), I still feel this big lump in my throat and I feel more bummed than ever. How can I live being this miserable?

What About It?

2. Is there anything wrong with Lisa wanting God to be her best friend? Why or why not?

3. Do you think having God as your best friend would eliminate the need for an "earthly" best friend? Why or why not?

Overlook an offense and bond a friendship;
fasten on to a slight and—good-bye, friend!
A quiet rebuke to a person of good sense
does more than a whack on the head of a fool.
Proverbs 17:9-10

What About This?

4. Describe a time when a friend hurt your feelings. How did you react to it?

5. Have you ever had problems forgiving a friend or had a friend who refused to forgive you? If so, how did this affect the friendship?

My Friend, My Mirror

Good friends can be like mirrors sometimes. They can reflect back to you who you really are—because you don't always see the real you. Sometimes this feels great, because a good friend will point out what you have going for you—qualities you may have overlooked. She might tell you that you have beautiful teeth, or that you're the kindest person she knows, or that your hair looks great when it's up. The problem is, it can go the other way too. A friend can point out your flaws. And even if she's right, it doesn't feel so good. Your friend might hint that you're being selfish or stingy or stupid, and naturally you don't really like to hear that.

your RQ (reaction quotient)

Circle the letter by the answer that sounds most like you.

1. Your good friend says something that personally offends you. You:
    a. Sweep it under the rug since she's only human.
    b. Get mad and get even.
    c. Admit that it hurt and ask her why she said it.

2. Your friend promises to meet you at the mall but never shows. You:
    a. Accept that she's just like that and go shopping alone.
    b. Leave the mall in a huff and try to decide whether or not you'll speak to her again.
    c. Call her to see what the problem is.

3. Your best friend seems to be making the move on your crush. You:
   a. Ignore it and tell yourself she's a better catch for him anyway.
   b. Confront her in front of him and everyone and accuse her of being a guy stealer.
   c. Talk to her privately to see if she really likes him or is just being friendly.

4. A casual friend shares a juicy piece of gossip about a close friend. You:
   a. Act like it's no big deal; everyone gossips.
   b. Indignantly inform her that it's none of her freaking business.
   c. Ask how she would feel if someone repeated something like that about her.

5. Your best friend suddenly quits speaking to you. You:
   a. Try not to show that you're hurt.
   b. Tell her she's a pretty pathetic friend.
   c. Try to find out what's troubling her and see if it can be fixed.

6. Your close friend makes fun of you in front of your other friends. You:
   a. Act like you don't care.
   b. Make fun of her, only more so.
   c. Tell her in private how you feel when she acts that way.

7. Your best friend is obsessed with her new boyfriend, and you feel abandoned. You:
   a. Bide your time; they'll probably break up eventually anyway.

    b. Confront her and tell her she must choose — it's either you or the guy.

    c. Privately tell her that you miss her and are concerned for your friendship, then see how she reacts.

So, what's your R.Q.? What kind of a reactor are you? Are your answers mostly A, B, or C?

Mostly A's = Ms. Suppressive. You want to appear laid-back, but you're really acting like a doormat. Good friends treat each other as equals. You need to stand up for yourself (in love) and quit being afraid to get to the bottom of things. If any friendship is so fragile that it'll fall apart if you question anything, it's not much of a friendship to start with.

Mostly Bs = Ms. Aggressive. You are being way too harsh with your friends. You may think that you're just cutting through the crud and getting to the point, but the fact is, you're probably hurting your friends' feelings. Tone it down and ask God to help you to speak the truth with love. And don't forget to treat your friends with the same kind of respect that you expect from them.

Mostly Cs = Ms. Progressive. *Woohoo!* You're doing it right! Your goal is to progress in your friendships. You're building foundations of good communication, mutual trust, and loyalty. Your friendships will probably be solid and long lasting.

My dear, dear friends, if God loved us like this, we certainly
ought to love each other. No one has seen God, ever.
But if we love one another, God dwells deeply within us,
and his love becomes complete in us—perfect love!

1 John 4:11-12

what kind of friend are you?

Understanding your own personality type (in regard to friendship) can really help you in dealing with your friends. Here's a quick quiz to reveal the kind of friend you are. Circle the following statements that best describe you.

1. I'm a dependable friend; if I promise to do something, I follow through.
2. I expect my friends to be loyal to me no matter what.
3. I'm a little shy; I like my friends to make the first move.
4. I come up with fun and wacky ideas for things to do with my friends.
5. My friends say I have a good sense of humor.
6. I wait for my friends to call me first.
7. I like to plan things for my friends and then make sure they do them.
8. I love helping my friends out of jams.
9. I sometimes stay on the fringes of social activities.
10. I like to observe others before jumping in.
11. I'm usually the life of the party.

12. My friends think I can be bossy.

13. My friends say I'm easygoing.

14. My friends think I'm a show-off.

15. My friends think I can be moody.

16. I don't like it when my friends don't agree with my plans.

17. I can be friendly with the most obnoxious people.

18. I like to be where the action is.

19. My friends say I'm not always reliable.

20. Sometimes I prefer being by myself.

21. I'm a take-charge kind of friend.

22. My friends think I'm easily distracted.

23. I like to let someone else take the lead.

24. I like solving my friends' problems.

25. Some friends think I'm overly sensitive.

26. Some of my friends think I don't get involved enough.

27. My friends love having me around.

28. Some of my friends think I can be insensitive.

Now look below to see which of your answers fall into which category. And, remember, no one is strictly one personality type — you're probably a mix. But the point is to see some of your strengths and weaknesses as a friend. Also, you may begin to understand why certain personality types get along with certain other personality types — just one of the many reasons you choose the friends you do.

Phlegmatic. (Answers 1, 5, 6, 8, 10, 13, 17, 23, 26.) Phoebe Phlegmatic is the easygoing, happy, and very laid-back friend. Phoebe enjoys life and doesn't get overly excited. Friends like her sense of humor, and she keeps them laughing. She's consistent and caring. But her friends do accuse her of not getting involved, because she likes to sit back and watch others. When Phoebe joins in, though, she's competent and capable. She's a kind and gracious friend. She loves her friends and her friends love her.

Sanguine. (Answers 4, 5, 11, 14, 18, 19, 22, 27.) Suzie Sanguine is the life of the party, popular, and talkative. She's warm, fun, caring, responsive, passionate. Suzie sometimes hurts her friends' feelings when she speaks without thinking, and she's an extrovert who always has an opinion. Suzie is everyone's friend, but not extremely loyal. She lives for the moment, goes with the flow, gets distracted, and isn't totally reliable, but her friends forgive her because she's so much fun.

Choleric. (Answers 2, 7, 12, 16, 21, 24, 28.) Chloe Choleric is the practical, hard-working, and no-nonsense friend. She's self-sufficient and will do what it takes to get the job done, even if she plows down her friends in the process. She moves quickly, almost intuitively, makes a plan and follows it through. A born leader, Chloe's friends appreciate her smart and capable ways. But once she takes her stand, they have to watch out because Chloe will accomplish her goals through whatever means suit her. She's not a very sympathetic or sensitive friend. She'd rather solve your problems than send you packing. But when friends need someone to take charge, Chloe's the one.

Melancholic. (Answers 1, 3, 6, 9, 10, 15, 20, 23, 25.) Melanie Melancholic is the quiet friend. She systematically analyzes herself and everyone around her. Her moods can swing from extremely happy to gloomy and depressed. Some friends think she's snobby. Melanie tends to avoid crowds or hangs on the fringes as she quietly observes others. She has only a few friends, but she is extremely loyal. She knows how to hide her feelings and make sacrifices for others. She is the artist, writer, intellectual type. Her tongue can be sharp, but it's usually a cover-up for her very tender heart.

Love from the center of who you are; don't fake it.
Run for dear life from evil; hold on for dear life to good.
Be good friends who love deeply; practice playing second fiddle.

Romans 12:9-10

To Have a Friend Is to Be a Friend

Many friendships get ruined by selfishness. One friend expects too much from the other and before long, resentment sets in. The key to a good friendship is to learn to put your friend first. This doesn't mean that you let your friend push you around or talk you into doing something you shouldn't. It simply means that you love and respect her so much that you want her life to be really great, you want her to succeed, you want her relationship with God to be strong, and you're willing to do whatever it takes to help her.

Does this mean you neglect yourself in the process? Or that you don't do your homework so you can help with hers? Of course not! Jesus said, "Love others as you love yourself." If you stop loving and caring for yourself, you won't be much use to anyone. But becoming a good friend does mean focusing less on yourself and your own ambitions as you learn to get behind your friend and become her biggest cheerleader. And the payoff? Well, not only do you establish a really valuable friendship but you have also become a friend of great worth.

ways to show your friend you care

- Be a good listener even when you don't feel like it.
- Get to know her family and speak respectfully of them.
- Don't always let her be the first one to call.
- Be sensitive to her feelings.
- Plan a surprise party for her birthday.
- Don't be too quick to point out her flaws.
- Defend her if someone else puts her down.
- Point out her character strengths.
- Encourage her to try new things.
- Don't insist on your own way.
- Speak positively about her to others.
- Don't compete with her for guys.
- Point out her most attractive features.
- Don't compare yourself to her, or her to you.
- Respect her time; don't call too late.
- Respect her parents' rules.
- Encourage her to do what's right.
- Know her likes and dislikes.

Words to Live By

(Consider memorizing one of these.)

Friends come and friends go,

but a true friend sticks by you like family.

Proverbs 18:24

Friends love through all kinds of weather.

Proverbs 17:17

This is the very best way to love.

Put your life on the line for your friends.

John 15:13

Now that you've cleaned up your lives by following the truth,

love one another as if your lives depended on it.

1 Peter 1:22

Journal Your Thoughts

Choose one of these verses. Write about how you can apply that verse to a specific friendship.

My Friendship Goals

Take some of the things you've been challenged by in this chapter and form them into specific goals for yourself as a friend.

My Goals Are:

Pen a Prayer

Take a moment to write a prayer from your heart. Invite God to partner with you as you move to a new level in understanding friendship and in being a good friend.

May our dependably steady and warmly personal God develop maturity in you so that you get along with each other as well as Jesus gets along with us all.

Romans 15:5

how *sweet*
it can be

Let's see how inventive we can be in encouraging love and helping out,
not avoiding worshiping together as some do but spurring each other on,
especially as we see the big Day approaching.

Hebrews 10:24-25

$\mathcal{F}$ellowship is a whole new level of friendship. It's a deep relationship that you only experience with fellow believers — and when it's good, it is very, very good. But sometimes fellowship goes sideways, and then it's not so good.

The point of this chapter is to get some clues for how to keep your fellowship times on track, how to avoid pitfalls, and ways to repair relationships that have been hurt in a fellowship situation. But most of all, you'll be encouraged to appreciate all the rewards that good fellowship has to offer.

God knows that you need to be around believers, and it's his plan that you become committed to and involved in some sort of fellowship situation. Whether it's through church or youth group or a Bible study or some kind of campus ministry, he wants you connected with other believers.

> "Look at it this way. If someone has a hundred sheep and one of them wanders off, doesn't he leave the ninety-nine and go after the one? . . . Your Father in heaven feels the same way. He doesn't want to lose even one of these simple believers."
>
> Matthew 18:12,14

Maybe you've heard Jesus' story about a lost sheep (Matthew 18:12-14). Well, it's only natural that a shepherd gets seriously worried when a sheep slips away from the flock. He knows the lone sheep is in real danger from wolves, lions, or bears. But a sheep that remains within the security of the flock is protected. In other words, there really is safety in numbers.

The same is true with you. If you separate yourself from Christians, you put your entire walk with God at risk. You have no one around to encourage you, or pray for you, or warn you about the big bad wolf that's waiting around the next corner. So hang in there with fellowship and stay tight with God.

> I want you woven into a tapestry of love, in touch with everything there is to know of God. Then you will have minds confident and at rest, focused on Christ, God's great mystery.
>
> Colossians 2:2

Superglue Love

Fellowship without love is a formula for disaster. Because, think about it, you put a bunch of believers together for a time of "fellowship" and what do they really have in common? Besides their faith? What can keep the group from blowing apart?

Okay, imagine you've just stepped into a fellowship group for the first time. Maybe the leader takes you around and introduces you to some people. You meet Franz Frinkle, science geek, sitting in the corner. His hair looks like something straight out of the eighties and he's got a really gross zit in the center of his forehead. Across from him sits Ashley Slater, head cheerleader and perennial optimist. Then there's Lindsey Clark, the no-nonsense academic with absolutely no fashion sense, and she's staring at Lane Osborne, football star and every girl's crush. There are quite a few more characters, all with absolutely nothing in common. Except their faith.

So maybe you're wondering what can possibly hold this group of mixed nuts together. What can unify so many totally diversified people and make them want to come back for more? God's answer is *love* — only love can bond these individuals together.

And not the flaky human kind of love that's dependent on how you feel about a person's looks, personality, or social status. No, it takes a *God-sourced love* to get over all the differences and obstacles that any fellowship group is bound to have. But once you let God love others through you, something amazing happens — something unexpected and totally exciting. *Unity.* Because love truly is God's form of superglue. It's how he connects his people to each other. And nothing works quite like it.

lisa's story continues . . .

"Hey, Lisa!" yells a voice from behind me. I turn to see Glen Stanley, our youth group leader, jogging toward me.

"Hey, Glen," I say in a less-than-enthusiastic voice.

"Everything okay with you?" he asks as he pauses to catch his breath next to my car.

I shrug and glance away. "I guess."

"You guess?"

I turn back to look at him. He's adjusting his dark-framed glasses and peering at me curiously. "I'm okay," I finally say, hoping that will end this little interrogation.

"You don't seem okay to me." He puts a hand on my shoulder now. "Really, Lisa, what's up?"

And that just does it. Right there in the stupid church parking lot I begin to cry. Then next thing I know, Glen is hugging me and saying that whatever the problem is, it can't be that bad. "Nothing's too big for God, Lisa," he finally says as I pull away and wipe my tears on my sleeve.

"It's not that big a thing, really," I say trying to get myself back together. "I guess I'm just lonely."

"Lonely?"

I nod. "Yeah, I kind of decided that I don't need friends anymore."

"Don't need friends?" He looks incredulous. "You honestly think you can get by without friends, Lisa?"

"I thought it might be less painful."

"So how's it working for you?"

"Not so great . . ."

Now he frowns. "Does that mean I'm not your friend anymore?"

I kind of smile. "No, I guess you're still my friend, Glen."

"Did you and Shelby get into a fight?"

"Not exactly."

So then he coaxes the story out of me and I tell him everything I remember.

"It sounds like something is missing here, Lisa."

"What do you mean?"

"I mean, Shelby wouldn't just dump you like that without a reason. Are you sure you didn't do or say something to offend her?"

"I don't think so . . ."

"Well, have you asked her?"

"Asked her?"

He kind of laughs now. "You know, you have a responsibility to keep the communication open if you want to keep the friendship going."

"But what about her?"

"I'm not talking to her. I'm talking to you."

"Right."

"And as your youth pastor, I'm telling you that you need to talk to Shelby and find out what's at the bottom of this. And then I want you to report back to me."

"Is that an order?"

"It is."

"Okay." And here's the weird thing. I actually feel kind of relieved. I mean, not that I really enjoy being told what to do, but in this case it's okay.

"And one more thing," he continues. "Make sure you pray about it first, Lisa. Ask God to guide you with your words and how you talk to her."

I agree to do that, and even though I'm feeling pretty nervous about it since I haven't talked to Shelby — I mean really talked — in weeks, I'm just not sure what will happen.

1. How do you think Glen knew that Lisa was having problems?

2. How would you react if a Christian friend confronted you like this about a concern?

"If a fellow believer hurts you, go and tell him—work it out between the two of you. If he listens, you've made a friend."

Matthew 18:15

3. How comfortable are you telling someone that they've offended you? Why is that?

4. What steps would you take before confronting someone?

Trusting Your Leaders

Although fellowship can happen under all sorts of circumstances, and on all kinds of levels, it is often an offshoot of church or some other ministry. And this means there are leaders involved. Whether it's your minister, youth pastor, or whatever, someone is usually running the show. And while no leader is perfect, he or she should have the kind of leadership qualities you can respect.

This is the description given in 1 Timothy 3:1-7:

> A leader must be well-thought-of, committed to his wife, cool and collected, accessible, and hospitable. He must know what he's talking about, not be overfond of wine, not pushy but gentle, not thin-skinned, not money-hungry. He must handle his own affairs well, attentive to his own children and having their respect. For if someone is unable to handle his own affairs, how can he take care of God's church? He must not be a new believer, lest the position go to his head and the Devil trip him up. Outsiders must think well of him, or else the Devil will figure out a way to lure him into his trap.

That's pretty specific, and it should give you a sense of what you can generally expect from a leader. Not that you should be critical of your leaders or try to point out their flaws, but God wants you to be wise enough to know whether or not a leader should be leading. God doesn't want you being led down the wrong path by the wrong kind of leader.

So once you get to the place where you trust and respect your leaders, you might want to commit yourself to praying for these people. You'll also want to stay in good communication with them, and be willing to receive counsel and direction from them.

Getting Honest About Fellowship

5. Describe what you consider to be *real* fellowship.

6. Are you involved in any kind of fellowship? Why or why not?

7. If you could change something about your fellowship times, what would it be?

8. Are you comfortable saying what you honestly think and feel in fellowship situations? Why or why not?

9. How would you rate your fellowship leader on a scale of 1 to 10?

1	2	3	4	5	6	7	8	9	10
pathetic loser					okay for an older person				this person totally rocks!

Explain why you gave him or her this rating.

Humble Hearts

Nothing messes up good fellowship like pride, boasting, or comparing. As soon as a group gives into something like this, it will quickly fall apart. For instance, someone shares about how they "brought someone to the Lord," and she goes on and on about how God is using her. And then someone else feels the need to say something equally impressive, and before you know it you've got this show-and-tell mentality where everyone is trying to look better than everyone else.

The thing is, only God can bring someone to himself. And if good things are happening in your life, it's only because of God. Sure, it's great to give God the credit, but in the process you need to be able to admit that without him you are nothing. When the spirit of a fellowship group can practice real humility, and remember that life is not about impressing others, then the group will really begin to grow.

Jesus taught his followers to think more highly of others than themselves. He wants you to think like this too. He wants us all to have humble hearts and a willingness to serve others. He wants you to spend more time encouraging a friend than trying to make yourself look good. And the funny thing is that when you live like this, not only do you make God look good but it looks good on you too!

Be Honest . . .

10. Do I sometimes see fellowship time as a chance to look good in front of my Christian friends? If so, why is looking good such a big deal to me?

11. What can I pray for my youth-group leaders and Christian friends?

12. What can I do to make our fellowship times better for everyone?

13. Have I specifically asked God about his plans for me in regard to fellowship? Do I sense he is leading me right now? If so, in what way?

And be very careful around them so you don't lose out on what we've worked so diligently in together; I want you to get every reward you have coming to you. Anyone who gets so progressive in his thinking that he walks out on the teaching of Christ, walks out on God. But whoever stays with the teaching, stays faithful to both the Father and the Son.

2 John 1:8-9

For Better or Worse

Okay, you know that love is God's superglue for holding a fellowship group together, but what if you're not committed to using it in the first place? What if you're sort of so-so about fellowship, like you can take it or leave it? For any kind of group to succeed, it takes commitment on the part of everyone involved. And to make a commitment like this to a group, you must first make a commitment to God.

So, do you believe God wants you in fellowship? If your answer is yes, then you need to ask yourself what your level of commitment is to fellowship.

14. What practical steps can you take to make it a priority to stay involved in a fellowship group?

15. Describe the role you play in your fellowship group. Do you show up and participate? Or do you sit in the back row like Lisa did during the worship service?

16. On a scale of 1 to 10 (1 = never and 10 = always), how comfortable are you with sharing your ideas and input with a group?

Would you like to see that change?

Some people get caught in the judgmental trap in their fellowship groups. Maybe they look down on someone because (1) that person has really messed up, (2) that person is acting like a total jerk, or (3) they simply don't like that person. But real fellowship is meant to be a "safe haven" where you accept everyone — warts and all. It's a place where people can gather and share honestly without fear of judgment or criticism. It's a place for encouragement, prayer, uplifting, teaching, worshiping, and just plain loving.

But this doesn't mean you just ignore it if someone does something that seriously offends you. You simply deal with it in a scriptural way. You honestly confront that person (in love!!!) and tell him or her your concerns. If the person doesn't respond well (like they tell you to go blow), then you take a second person and confront them again (in love!!!). If that doesn't work, you get the youth-group leader involved.

Whatever you do, make sure you do it in love and with the kind of commitment that promises to go the distance with your fellow believers. Because for better or for worse, you've got all eternity to spend with them.

creative ways to fellowship

- Attend a sports event together and get really rowdy while cheering.
- Volunteer at the local senior center and sing them some songs.
- Do a Bible study bike ride where you stop every ten minutes to read a verse.
- Walk and talk (for spiritual and physical exercise).
- Start an online prayer group.

- Do a book club where you read a Christian novel and discuss it.
- Get a Christian friend to take on a new hobby with you.
- Start a small support group of Christian friends at school.
- Attend a missions conference together.
- Go to a Christian rock concert together.
- Take on a challenge together (a mountain climb, marathon).
- Plan a camping trip together.
- Watch silly old movies together.
- Learn to play a musical instrument together.

Words to Live By

(Consider memorizing one of these.)

You use steel to sharpen steel,
and one friend sharpens another.
Proverbs 27:17

They committed themselves to the teaching of the apostles, the life
together, the common meal, and the prayers.
Acts 2:42

Dear friend, when you extend hospitality to Christian brothers and sisters,
even when they are strangers, you make the faith visible.
3 John 1:5

Journal Your Thoughts

Choose one of the verses above. How does it apply to your own personal fellowship situation? How does it encourage you to do something more?

My Fellowship Goals

Now it's time to write down your specific goals for improving your fellowship life. Glance back over this chapter to see what stands out to you. Then write your goals below.

My Goals Are:

Fellowship Final

17. Is there really any good excuse to avoid fellowship? Why or why not?

18. Have you ever considered taking more leadership in your fellowship group? Why or why not?

19. Do you have a good relationship with your youth group or fellowship leader? Why or why not? And what could improve it?

20. Write a prayer, asking God to lead you in the whole fellowship arena. Invite him to challenge you to a deeper commitment to both him and your fellowship group.

But if we walk in the light, God himself being the light,

we also experience a shared life with one another,

as the sacrificed blood of Jesus, God's Son, purges all our sin.

1 John 1:7

he's the
one!

GOD said, "It's not good for the Man to be alone;
I'll make him a helper, a companion."
Genesis 2:18

ost girls spend more time than they'll admit to daydreaming about the "right" guy — *the one*! And that's only natural. God designed you with a built-in desire to hook up with a guy who is absolutely perfect for you. Unfortunately, too many girls think it's time to hook up way sooner than what God has planned. And that usually leads to heartache and suffering.

Running ahead of God is never good, but in the area of romantic relationships it almost always turns out bad. Even so, people do it all the time. It's like an epidemic! Okay, that might be partially a result of the culture we live in. You can't watch TV or a movie or read a magazine without having dating, romance, love, and more specifically *sex* thrown literally right in your face. Between reality TV, the Internet, and rock stars who practically do it while they sing, you can become so saturated with these messages that you eventually give in to that kind of thinking. But is that God's kind of thinking? Does he really want you to be obsessed with hooking up with a guy, getting in over your head, and eventually being tempted to have sex before you're married? Of course not. And that's because God, your loving Father, knows that this mentality only sets you up for getting hurt.

Maybe you've already experienced some of this. Perhaps you've been in a relationship where you thought the guy was truly "the one," maybe you even made promises to each other, and maybe you gave yourself completely over to him (body and soul), but in the end the love fizzled out and someone got hurt. Maybe even you.

But even if that's the case, you can learn from those things, get smarter, and not make the same mistake again and again and again. Or maybe you think the only way you learn is from the school of hard knocks. If that's the case, you might as well know that it's going to cost you something down the line. And there will undoubtedly come a day when you'll look back with huge regrets and wish that you'd done it all differently.

Because romance—*real romance*—is so worth waiting for! It's so much sweeter when you cooperate with God's plan and timing, and *then* Mr. Perfect comes along. And you realize, "This is the guy I've been waiting for—and he's so glad I waited!" And that's when you understand that God really did know what he was up to all along.

I know what I'm doing. I have it all planned out—
plans to take care of you, not abandon you,
plans to give you the future you hope for.
Jeremiah 29:11

1. If you really, really, really believe what Jeremiah 29:11 says, how would that affect your choices regarding guys in high school?

Dating Game or Waiting Game?

To date or not to date, *that* is the question. Is it better for you to completely put aside dating until you reach an age where a serious courtship is an actual option? Or is it better to get to know guys, go out on group dates, and find out what you really want in a boyfriend?

Unfortunately, there is no absolute black-and-white answer that works for everyone. The good news is, that makes this one of those things where you can't judge or criticize someone for their choice — God may be telling one person it's okay to date and telling another to wait. He knows what's best for everyone — and since everyone is different, his answers are different too.

So whether or not you date, like so many other decisions, is really between you and God. And only God, your loving Father, can show you what's the very best for you. But if you ask him, he *will* show you. He might speak through your parents, or church, or friends, or his Word, or even that quiet voice deep inside you. But trust him, he will speak. The question is, will you listen?

It's really hard to hear what God's saying when you feel yourself attracted to a certain guy. It's easy to get confused with things like emotions and hormones, not to mention peer pressure hammering at you. So how can you know whether or not you should be dating this guy?

Okay, if you believe you've met the right guy and think it's okay to date but aren't completely sure, try giving yourself the following test.

1. Is this guy a fellow believer?
2. Is this guy involved in a church?
3. Do we have lots of common interests?
4. Does this guy want what's best for me?
5. Does this guy ever tempt me to compromise my commitment to purity?
6. Does this guy respect my family and their values?
7. Does my family like and respect this guy?
8. Do my friends approve of this guy?
9. Does it improve my relationship with God to date this guy?
10. Do I believe God wants me to date this guy?

If you answered "yes!" to all of these questions, it's probably okay to date this guy. If not, you should reconsider.

lisa's story continues . . .

I thank Glen for his advice and get into my car and just sit there. I know I could possibly catch Shelby coming out to the parking lot, but then I remember she's with Mattie and realize this is probably not the best time for this conversation. Besides, I haven't done what Glen said yet. I haven't prayed for God to lead me in this.

So I drive home, go to my room, play with my kitten, and eventually I get around to praying for God's help in this.

"Help me to know what to say to Shelby," I pray. "And help me not to sound too mad at her. Most of all, just help me to find out why she's

treating me like this and then, if I need to, help me to move on."

I finally call her cell phone in the afternoon. I halfway expect to get her voice messaging, which might be a relief, but to my surprise she picks up and I am stuttering to tell her why I'm calling.

"I want to talk to you," I finally manage to say.

"What's up?" she asks.

"I just need to talk, but I don't really want to do it on the phone."

"Well, I just dropped Mattie at her house. Want me to swing by?"

"You don't mind?"

"Not really." But even as she says this, her voice sounds a little tight, like something is still wrong between us and, of course, I know that it is.

So we agree for her to come here, and suddenly I'm feeling really nervous. I go around straightening my already neater-than-usual room (result of all my solitary confinement), and I try to keep praying, but mostly I'm just repeating myself. And suddenly she's here, she's sitting in the chair by my desk and holding Clarice in her lap, and I know it's time to say whatever it is that I need to say.

"Look," I begin — wishing I hadn't said 'look.' "I know something is wrong. I mean, I realize that we haven't been talking and stuff, and I guess I was wondering if maybe I did something, well, something to offend you."

She looks up at me with raised brows. "You mean you don't know?"

"Huh?"

"What you did? You don't know what you did?"

I shrug. "Not really."

"Really?" she looks totally unconvinced.

"Really. I have no idea what you're talking about."

"Okay, tell me you don't remember telling Tina Millagro something

about me a few weeks ago, back when I first started going out with Peter?"

"Tina Millagro?" I frown now. "I hardly ever talk to her."

"Well, you talked to her back then."

I try to remember, and then it hits me. "You mean in youth group that time you didn't come and I was kind of mad at you?"

"That'd be the time."

And it hits me. I did say something to Tina. I was in a snit because Shelby had, at the last minute, decided to go out with Peter instead of going to youth group with me. I never did like going by myself.

"Where's Shelby?" Tina asked me that night when I showed up alone.

"Out with Peter the heathen," I said back. Well, naturally Tina thought that was hilarious, and then she got me going about it, and I suppose I really shot off my mouth. And, of course, Tina's mouth is even bigger than mine. She probably told Shelby the very next day. Stupid, stupid, stupid me!

"I'm sorry," I finally say to Shelby. "I guess I forgot all about that."

"Well, I didn't."

"Obviously."

"Did you mean all that stuff, Lisa? About how you thought I was falling away from the Lord and how Peter was a bad influence and how I was changing so much?"

I shrug. "I might have sort of meant it, at the time. I mean, I was kind of hurt and I probably exaggerated stuff. But I was a little worried about you getting involved with Peter. I mean, he's not a Christian."

"But he's a nice guy."

"I know." I look down at the pillow sitting in my lap and feel like I'm about two inches tall. Then I look back at Shelby. "I really am sorry. The main reason I said all that crud was because I missed you. I didn't want to share you with Peter . . . and then you and Mattie started hanging together . . . and then it seemed like I really did lose you — " I hear my voice crack now and I really, really don't want to cry. "And, well," I manage, "I miss you and I wish we could still be friends. But I'll understand if you — "

Then Shelby jumps up and gives me a big hug with Clarice right in between us. "Of course, I want to be friends. But what you said hurt me."

"Why didn't you tell me then?" I ask when we finally step apart.

She shrugs. "Just stubborn, I guess. Maybe I was hoping you'd make the first move, and when you didn't, well, I just decided to move on — kind of to teach you a lesson."

Then it's like the ice between us has melted and she's telling me about what's going on between her and Peter, and I have to bite my tongue to keep from saying anything because it sounds to me like Shelby is getting in way over her head. But I'm so glad to have her friendship back that I don't say anything negative about Peter.

No test or temptation that comes your way is beyond the course of what others have had to face. All you need to remember is that God will never let you down; he'll never let you be pushed past your limit; he'll always be there to help you come through it.

1 Corinthians 10:13

What's Up with This?

2. Has a romantic relationship ever tempted you to go too far? If so, what happened?

3. How do you handle it when temptation hits you?

4. Have you asked God how far is too far? Do you honor the limitations he gives you? Why or why not?

Boy Crazy Is Nuts

What Shelby is telling Lisa is that she and Peter have been pushing the boundaries in their physical relationship and it's making her a little nervous. But at the same time, she's really excited. She thinks "Peter is definitely the one" and she's totally in love with him. She's even considering abandoning the abstinence pledge that she and Lisa made several years ago. Lisa is shocked and concerned, but now she's more worried about preserving the friendship than speaking her opinions. What should she do?

Between the two of them, Shelby was the one who'd always been a little boy crazy. She'd gone with a number of guys and almost always ended up getting hurt when they broke up. Lisa thought it had something to do with the fact that Shelby's father wasn't much of a dad, but she'd never said as much.

Everyone knows someone who's "boy crazy" — the kind of girl who goes from one relationship straight into the next. This girl is never comfortable being without a guy — it's as if she thinks her value is all wrapped up in having a boyfriend by her side. And maybe you're asking, what's wrong with that? The problem is that a lot of boys know how to take advantage of a girl like that — it's like they radar into her neediness and know how to make it work for their benefit. And, whether you want to admit or not, most guys between the ages of sixteen and eighteen are mainly interested in one thing — and like it or not, that's sex. It's as if all their hormones are firing and cross-firing at the same time, and they can't help but think about sex — a lot! Some estimates say that guys in this age group think about sex every few minutes.

Maybe that's what makes dating in high school such a precarious thing for some people. It's like, why would you take a girl who's dressed like Britney Spears and leave her alone with a guy whose hormones are already pumped and not expect them to run into some problems? It just doesn't make sense. And yet for millions of teens, this is a way of life. Is it any surprise that teen pregnancy and STD statistics are at an all-time high? And here's another statistic — a lot of those pregnant teen girls are still wearing their True Love Waits rings. They were so certain that they were practicing abstinence that they never learned to take any birth-control precautions, and then they are pregnant.

So maybe you're starting to see that some kinds of dating and boy-craziness are pretty nuts. Maybe the next quiz will help you see where you fit into the whole dating game thing.

what's your DQ?

Okay, this isn't about ice cream. So circle the statements that best represent how you feel, and you'll soon know what your D.Q. (dating quotient) really is.

1. I think about guys constantly.
2. I want a boyfriend who likes doing outdoor stuff.
3. I'm involved in lots of activities.
4. I have several good guy friends.
5. I dress to get guys' attention — the sexier the better.
6. I like it when my girlfriends compliment me on my clothes.
7. I don't mind that I've never had a serious boyfriend.
8. I have posters of hot guys in my room.
9. I'd rather have fun than fuss with my hair.
10. I love having my girlfriends over just to hang with.
11. I've had a lot of boyfriends in the past.
12. My grades are pretty consistent.
13. I spend a lot of time on my appearance; I like to look really good.
14. I'm open to having a boyfriend.

15. My parents have an okay marriage.

16. My girlfriends and I love to go shopping.

17. Some of my friends have a steady guy.

18. I get distracted by guys in class.

19. My friends and I date occasionally, like dances and stuff.

20. I watch a lot of TV and movies.

21. My friends and I like dating in groups.

22. My marriage will be way better than what my parents ever had.

23. I expect my boyfriend to give me a lot of attention.

24. I like to read really good books.

25. I have pictures of my friends in my room.

26. I don't want to be tied down to just one guy.

27. All my friends have boyfriends.

28. I like playing video games.

29. I would like a marriage similar to what my parents have.

30. I enjoy doing sports with a mix of guys and girls.

See which numbers you circled and what category they mostly fit into to find out what your D.Q. really is. Remember, this is only a silly quiz, and you may not fall completely into one category.

Totally boy crazy! (Answers 1, 5, 8, 11, 13, 18, 20, 22, 23, 27.) You think you cannot survive without a boyfriend. Everything in your life seems to revolve around guys. Unfortunately, this is probably a case of too much too soon, and you may someday regret being nuts over guys.

Boys make cool friends. (Answers 2, 4, 9, 14, 15, 17, 21, 25, 26, 28, 30.) You're comfortable hanging with guys for the fun of it. And that's great, but you still need to remember a guy can really be attracted to a laid-back girl like you, so watch out for the guy who will try to take advantage of you.

Girls just want to have fun. (Answers 3, 6, 7, 10, 12, 16, 19, 21, 24, 25, 26, 29, 30.) You're cool with that. You enjoy life and your friends, and if guys fit in, that's okay. If not, you're still having a good time. Way to go!

Guy Friends vs. Boyfriends

So maybe you're rethinking the dating thing. Maybe you're ready to consider some other options. Or maybe you're just tired of the pressure of being alone on a date, having to come up with things to talk about one-on-one, or trying to extract yourself from a compromising position when your date suddenly wants to "have some fun."

How about getting to know guys as friends? By doing things in groups without pairing off, you can spend time with several girl and guy friends and just enjoy getting to know each other. You see people for who they are when they're interacting with a group. And bowling or miniature golf might sound silly, but it's actually pretty fun when you've got a bunch of friends doing it together.

Another good thing about having guy friends vs. boyfriends is that it teaches you to be comfortable around guys without feeling like it has to develop into something more. You begin to know and understand that guys, like girls, have some pretty deep feelings and can even carry on interesting conversations. They might not admit this to their macho guy friends, but most guys don't like the constant pressure of the whole dating, love, and sex thing. The truth is, guys also want to have fun. So why not have some good clean fun as a group?

Ask Yourself . . .

5. Am I comfortable with my attitude toward guys? Why or why not?

6. Is my dating (or nondating) life pleasing to God? Why or why not?

7. What are the qualities I want to have in a husband someday?

8. What qualities do I think my future husband will be looking for in me?

9. How am I doing on the qualities I just listed?

> Trust GOD from the bottom of your heart;
> don't try to figure out everything on your own.
> Listen for GOD's voice in everything you do, everywhere you go;
> he's the one who will keep you on track.
>
> Proverbs 3:5-6

What About This?

10. Have you asked God to direct you when it comes to your relationships with guys? Why or why not?

11. Do you think God can really "keep you on track" in a dating relationship? Why or why not?

12. Write any questions you'd like to ask God about dating in general or about a particular guy.

13. Who can help you hear God's voice in response to these questions?

Can't Do It Alone

Okay, maybe you're sensing that God is calling you to something higher when it comes to guys and dating. Maybe you're even considering making or renewing some promises or pledges to God about things like purity, dating, abstinence. But sometimes you just feel so weak, you're not sure if you can really stick to your word, and you hate making a promise you can't keep.

God does not expect you to do this alone. For one thing, he wants to go with you. He wants to strengthen you, protect you, and guide you. But he also wants you to surround yourself with strong Christian friends who can do the same. Maybe one good reason for trials like this is to teach you to depend on God and your Christian sisters and brothers for help and strength when you need it. And you can return the favor when they're struggling.

Words to Live By

(Consider memorizing one of these.)

"Stay alert; be in prayer so you don't wander into temptation without even knowing you're in danger. There is a part of you that is eager, ready for anything in God. But there's another part that's as lazy as an old dog sleeping by the fire."

Matthew 26:41

Don't let anyone under pressure to give in to evil say, "God is trying to trip me up." God is impervious to evil, and puts evil in no one's way. The temptation to give in to evil comes from us and only us. We have no one to blame but the leering, seducing flare-up of our own lust.

James 1:13-14

Journal Your Thoughts

Choose one of these verses. What is God saying to your heart through those words?

My Guy Goals

Do you have a clearer idea of what God has for you now in regard to guys and dating? Glance over some of the previous pages and see what stands out. Then create some specific goals (personal to you) that will be a guideline for how you will interact with guys in the future.

My Goals Are:

Final Thoughts on Love, Romance, and Marriage

14. Do I really believe God has someone for me? What do I think he'll be like?

15. How can I learn to trust God to bring Mr. Perfect along in his timing, not mine?

16. Is God calling me to make a special commitment to him in regard to my personal purity, sexual abstinence, or dating in general? If so, what is it?

17. Write a prayer that's a heartfelt promise to God. Tell him that you want to live life his way and not yours.

There's more to come: We continue to shout our praise even when we're hemmed in with troubles, because we know how troubles can develop passionate patience in us, and how that patience in turn forges the tempered steel of virtue, keeping us alert for whatever God will do next.

Romans 5:3-4

the big
outreach

Go easy on those who hesitate in the faith.

Go after those who take the wrong way.

Be tender with sinners, but not soft on sin.

The sin itself stinks to high heaven.

Jude 1:22-23

What About This?

1. Describe what you think it means to "be tender with sinners, but not soft on sin."

2. How would you go about doing this with a friend of yours?

Okay, this book is about relationships, and some of the most challenging relationships can be with unbelievers. But they can also be the most rewarding. Unfortunately, this is an area where many Christians get confused. For instance, some Christians believe they should "separate themselves from unbelievers" — almost as if they're afraid the unsaved person will contaminate them or drag them down. But that's not what Jesus did, and it's not what he taught either. Jesus spent serious time with unbelievers without allowing them to negatively influence him. He wants us to do the same. The trick is knowing when and who and how much time. That's where God comes in.

Hopefully, this chapter will widen your perspective about reaching out to others, and maybe you'll even pick up some tools for doing it. Because although this section is the last and shortest one, this topic is one of God's top priorities for you. He wants to use your life to touch people who are hurting or searching or lonely.

"I [Jesus] was hungry and you fed me,

I was thirsty and you gave me a drink,

I was homeless and you gave me a room,

I was shivering and you gave me clothes,

I was sick and you stopped to visit,

I was in prison and you came to me. . . .

"I'm telling the solemn truth:

Whenever you did one of these things

to someone overlooked or ignored,

that was me—you did it to me."

Matthew 25:35-36,40

What Does This Mean?

3. Jesus tells his followers that when they visit an overlooked person in prison, they're really visiting him. How can that be?

4. What does that have to do with you?

5. Describe a time when you helped someone. How did that make you feel? How do you think it made God feel?

God's Hands

You are God's hands—the way he reaches out and helps others, gives a gentle touch or a needed hug. The way unbelievers see and experience God is mostly through you and others who live their lives for him. In other words, *people are watching you.* Now instead of feeling pressured by this newsbreak, remember that God doesn't want you doing these things on your own strength—he wants to do these things *through* you. Just make sure you're doing all you can to be available. And stay tightly connected to him. Because while you're God's hands, he's everything else, and without him those hands are just lifeless and empty.

lisa's story continues . . .

It's been just a week since Shelby and I returned to being best friends. And while Mattie's still in the picture, I can see that she and Shelby were never that close. For one thing, Mattie, despite visiting our church, is uninterested in becoming a Christian. She thinks she's "good enough as is"—those were her exact words. Still, I'm praying for her and trying to remain a friend to her.

But honestly, it's Shelby who's got me worried. And finally I just have to say something. I only pray that I say it right. I wait until after school.

She needs a ride because her old beater car's in the shop again. I invite her to get coffee and then bring up the subject of Peter once we're seated. And trust me, I've been praying and praying about the words I'm going to speak.

"I'm concerned about you and Peter," I begin with some hesitation.

She takes in a sharp breath then waits. "What?" she finally says.

"Well…" I sigh. "I know you really think you love him and everything, but have you stopped to ask God whether or not Peter's really the one for you?"

She actually seems to consider this as she stirs her latte. Then she shrugs.

"I mean, you're such a cool girl, Shelby, and I really think God has great things for you, including a relationship that will really make you happy—"

"And your point is?"

"You don't really seem that happy with Peter. I mean, I know you really like him, but you seem stressed out a lot of the time. And it's usually after you guys have had a serious date, if you know what I mean."

She nods and looks down.

"And if Peter really was God's choice for you, it seems like you'd be happy and you wouldn't be so uptight and—"

"You're right, Lisa." She looks up and her eyes are bright with tears. "It's not working with Peter. He keeps pushing and pushing me to go further and further, and I know I can't keep holding him off. And sometimes, after a date, I feel so cruddy and yucky, and it's like I can't even talk to God about it."

"Do you know why that is?"

She uses the napkin to catch a tear that's streaking down her cheek.

"It might be that God doesn't want me with Peter. I guess I've suspected that for a while, but I just never really thought about it too much."

"So what are you going to do now?"

"I don't know . . ."

"Are you going to keep dating him?"

She frowns now. "I'm not sure . . . we were supposed to go out again tomorrow."

"But if it's like you say, Shelby . . . well, maybe you should — " Then I stop myself. Or maybe it's God that's stopping me.

"What?" she says in a slightly defensive tone. "Are you going to tell me to break up with him?"

I shake my head no. "I guess I'd just encourage you to ask God about this. He's the only one who knows what you need to do."

"But maybe I can keep things from going too far," she says quickly. "And besides, I keep thinking that Peter might come to God through me. I've even invited him to church."

"Maybe . . ."

"But you're not convinced."

"You're the one who needs to figure this out, Shelby. I'm just here to be your friend."

"Okay, okay, tell me, Lisa. Honestly, what do you think I should do?"

I consider this carefully then say, "Maybe you should ask yourself if dating Peter is helping or hurting your relationship with God."

She looks uncomfortable, but finally answers. "Hurting . . ."

"So, I guess you'll have to ask God to show you what to do."

She nods. "Thanks, Lisa. You're a good friend."

What About This?

6. Lisa doesn't come out and tell Shelby what to do in regard to Peter. Do you think this is right or wrong? Why?

7. How would you deal with an unsaved friend who was really blowing it?

> Now that I've put you there on a hilltop, on a light stand—shine!
> Keep open house; be generous with your lives.
> By opening up to others, you'll prompt people to
> open up with God, this generous Father in heaven.
>
> Matthew 5:16

Just Be Yourself

Some people think "evangelizing" means you have to reinvent yourself in order to step up to the task. But that's ridiculous. Why would God make you the way he did if he wanted you to become someone else? What God wants is willing hearts who aren't afraid to be themselves. That means being honest and open about who you are and the fact that you aren't perfect — just forgiven. What you have to offer others isn't a formula for a perfect, easy, happy little life. But if you're transparent, you should be able to show them that, yes, you're still human, you still struggle, but at least you have God's help now. Not only that, but you have things like peace and hope and direction. And those are some pretty attractive things to someone who's still struggling to figure things out.

So don't be afraid to be who you are, and don't try to put on the appearance of having it all together — that just turns most people off anyway.

What's Your Style?

8. Are you comfortable telling others about what God's doing in your life? Why or why not?

9. Do you think God's presence in your life is something that others can see, even when you're not speaking up? Why or why not?

10. Who has been most influential in your walk with God? Why?

11. What's your favorite way to help someone?

Availability Beats Ability

Some people may know the Bible cover to cover. They may have polished speaking skills and great confidence in sharing the gospel with others but never do it. God isn't looking for the ability as much as availability. If he can speak through a donkey (Old Testament) he can surely speak through you. But only if you're willing. He won't force himself on anyone.

So instead of freaking over whether or not you know exactly where 2 Thessalonians is, why not just say, "Here I am, God. Use me." Then see what happens.

With pure heart, clear head, steady hand; in gentleness, holiness, and honest love; when we're telling the truth, and when God's showing his power; when we're doing our best setting things right . . .

2 Corinthians 6:6-7

lisa's story wraps up

I am relieved to say that Shelby (after subjecting herself to one grueling date when she almost had to call for help) broke up with Peter. Even Mattie was glad.

"Shelby told me what you said to her," Mattie says as we wait for Shelby to join us in the lunch line. "I think that was pretty cool."

"Seriously?" I study Mattie. "I thought you weren't into the God thing."

"I mean it's cool that you didn't like preach at her or get mad or tell her what to do or anything. She said you were really sweet about it." Then Mattie laughed. "Not like me. I'd already read her the riot act and told her she was being a total idiot. Everyone knows Peter is smooth, but he's after one thing, and once he gets it, well, the girl's history. But would she listen to me?"

"She wouldn't?"

"No way. But I'm glad she listened to you. I really didn't want to see her get hurt."

Then Shelby is joining us, and for some reason I feel more hopeful than ever — not just about my friendship with Shelby, but also with what might be ahead for Mattie. Mostly I just feel hopeful about what God has in store for my life. It's gonna be great!

ways to reach out

- Smile at someone you don't know.
- Offer to help someone with something you're good at.
- Buy somebody lunch — hopefully someone who needs it.
- Comfort someone who seems down.

- Volunteer at the local soup kitchen or senior center.
- Compliment someone who lacks confidence.

Words to Live By

(Consider memorizing one of these.)

> "Here's another way to put it: You're here to be light,
> bringing out the God-colors in the world.
> God is not a secret to be kept.
> We're going public with this, as public as a city on a hill."
>
> Matthew 5:14

> "If I make you light-bearers, you don't think I'm going to
> hide you under a bucket, do you?
> I'm putting you on a light stand."
>
> Matthew 5:15

Journal Your Thoughts

Choose one of the verses above. Carefully consider the meaning and write below what it means to you.

My Reach~Out Goals

Ask God to give you at least one specific thing that you can do to make yourself more available to God and others. Write your goal(s) below.

My Goals Are:

A Reach-Out Prayer

Write a prayer for how you want God to use you in reaching out to others and creating new relationships.

"God authorized and commanded me to commission you:
Go out and train everyone you meet, far and near, in this way of life,
marking them by baptism in the threefold name:
Father, Son, and Holy Spirit.
Then instruct them in the practice of all I have commanded you.
I'll be with you as you do this, day after day after day,
right up to the end of the age."

Matthew 28:18-20

author

Melody Carlson has written dozens of books for all age groups, but she particularly enjoys writing for teens. Perhaps this is because her own teen years remain so vivid in her memory. After claiming to be an atheist at the ripe old age of twelve, she later surrendered her heart to Jesus and has been following him ever since. Her hope and prayer for all her readers is that each one would be touched by God in a special way through her stories. For more information , visit Melody's website at www.melodycarlson.com.

DISCOVER A UNIQUE NEW KIND OF BIBLE STUDY.

How did Jesus teach many of his most important lessons? He told stories. That's the idea behind the first series of Bible studies from best-selling fiction author Melody Carlson. In each of the four studies, Melody weaves fictional stories with practical discussion questions to get you thinking about some of the most important topics in life: your relationship with God, your relationship with others, identity, and forgiveness.

Knowing God Better Than Ever
978-1-57683-725-2

Finding Out Who You Really Are
978-1-57683-726-9

Discovering a Forgiveness Plan
978-1-57683-728-3

Visit your local Christian bookstore,
call NavPress at 1-800-366-7788, or log on to www.navpress.com
to purchase.

To locate a Christian bookstore near you,
call 1-800-991-7747.